Guerrilla Networking

Guerrilla Networking

The Best Way to Capture
and Keep Great Jobs

Robert T. Uda, MBA, MS, BS^2

Served on over 75 boards, councils, directorships, and panels

iUniverse, Inc.
New York Lincoln Shanghai

Guerrilla Networking
The Best Way to Capture and Keep Great Jobs

iUniverse books may be ordered through booksellers or by contacting:

iUniverse
2021 Pine Lake Road, Suite 100
Lincoln, NE 68512
www.iuniverse.com
1-800-Authors (1-800-288-4677)

Because of the dynamic nature of the Internet, any Web addresses or links contained in this book may have changed since publication and may no longer be valid.

The views expressed in this work are solely those of the author and do not necessarily reflect the views of the publisher, and the publisher hereby disclaims any responsibility for them.

ISBN: 978-0-595-47949-8

Printed in the United States of America

Dedication

Guerrilla Networking is dedicated to all job seekers who know how to be outstanding networking nodes.

Contents

Preface

Guerrilla Networking provides you with networking principles, strategies, and tactics that you apply in an employment or job search to maximize your job searching results. It includes provocative secrets and ideas for employment and career networking. *Guerrilla Networking* opens eyes, causes outside-of-the-box thinking, and promulgates paradigm shifts.

Guerrilla Networking: The Best Way to Capture and Keep Great Jobs works hand-in-hand with six of Uda's other related career development books. They are as follows:

- *Everything is Negotiable: Achieving Your True Worth by Successfully Negotiating*

- *Career Quest for Young Professionals: How to Maintain a Competitive Edge Over Your Peers*

- *Career Quest for College Graduates: Developing a Successful Career by Leveraging Each of Your Jobs*

- *Career Quest for College Students: Career Development for Those Who Plan to Have a Successful Career*

- *Resumes That Pack a Punch! Creating Beefy Bullets That Grab, Hook, and Wow Hiring Managers into Calling You for an Interview*

- *What Hue Is Your Bungee Cord? Job Searching Strategies for Those Over 40 Years of Age*

If you learn, internalize, and apply the principles contained in this book, you will capture and keep good jobs throughout your career.

If you disagree with anything that I have written in this book, I encourage you to write me and voice your disagreement. I always like to hear and learn about other people's views on whatever I write. Never do I believe that I know all truth on anything. I am always willing to change my views if someone presents contrary responses that make sense to me. That being said, I look forward to hearing from you.

All writings and opinions in this book are solely mine. Any error would be my error only. If you find errors, please bring them to my attention. We will correct them in subsequent editions of this book. I hope you enjoy the real-life stories in this book as I thoroughly have enjoyed living and writing about them. Thank you.

Robert T. Uda
San Marcos, California
January 2008

Chapter 1
Guerrilla Networking — Motivation

*I*t is estimated that over 80 percent of jobs are found through personal net-working rather than help wanted ads. Your use of networking groups will not only broaden your contacts but will also enable you to strengthen your verbal communication skills for those all important job interviews.[1]

Steven Rothberg

Net-centric Warfare — Strategic Networking

Networking is the most important of all of your strategies to use for capturing a good job. People acquire most good jobs through effective networking. Do a lot of networking, but limit it to strategic networking. In other words, don't waste your valuable time networking with every Tom, Dick, Harry, and GI Joe around. Network with those nodes you want to cultivate and keep on your net-working matrix. A node is a contact individual on your network. You can find good jobs through your good nodes on your network.

> **Uda Bomb # 1**
>
> *Networking is the most important of all of your strategies to use for capturing a good job.*

---

[1] Steven Rothberg, "The Value of Networking with Alumni," *Networking Resources.* (North Chelmsford, MA, Net-Temps, Inc., http://www.net-temps.com/ 2004), visit Steven's website at http://www.CollegeRecruiter.com.

1

Two-way Comm—Quid Pro Quo

Remember, whenever any of your networking nodes does something for you, you should feel obligated to return the favor and do something for him or her. Networking is a two-way street. It is an "If you'll scratch my back, I'll scratch your back" arrangement. Lawyers call that a *quid pro quo* arrangement.

Networking should be viewed as a business transaction, says [an East Coast management] consultant, which drives a specialized economy of favors. "The deal is, I give you a favor, you owe me a favor." Each exchange of favors is supposed to preserve a mutually advantageous system of informal communication, not establish an interpersonal relationship, he says. Moreover, both sides must hold up their end for the system to remain healthy.[2]

Survival Training—Leeches or Bloodsuckers

If someone repeatedly asks you for help but never gives any help in return but screws you instead, drop that person from your network. With friends like that, who needs enemies? I've had some students like that. They just take and take and take but never return anything. I don't call them networking nodes. Instead, I call them leeches or bloodsuckers.

Incommunicado—No Response for Help

Mind you, I will help all of my students at any time at no cost during the semester that they take my course. What I'm concerned about are students who graduate and then months to years later write me an email and ask me to review and redline their attached resume. Of course, I gladly do it. But then, sometimes I get a thanks, yet many times I don't even get a response at all!

---

[2]   Douglas B. Richardson, "Why Women Make Better Networkers," *CareerJournal.com*. Extracted on 4/16/07 from http://www.careerjournal.com.

Dud Bombs—Network Nulls not Nodes

All I would expect them to do in return is to spend less than $15 to purchase a book of mine like this one for example. But they won't even do that! I may spend an hour or more carefully redlining their resume, which would cost a client at least $100 for me to redline a resume. But would these leeches spend a measly 15 bucks to buy my book? No! Would you like to have someone like that on your network? I don't think so.

World Domination—Job of Your Dreams

What are the best ways to find the job of your dreams?

Patton: "Americans Love to Fight"—Find Your Passion

You first need to determine your passion. Your passion is what motivates you, what drives you, and what moves you to action without any prompting from anyone. People marvel at my ability to write and publish another book every six months on average. I don't need to push myself to do it. Writing is my passion. I write several pages for my books every day. I've been disciplined to do that. It's a habit.

Career Fit—Match Job to Your Passion

You need to identify the jobs that are of your dreams, the industry they are in, and the companies these jobs are in. Go on the *Internet* to the major job searching sites (such as Monster.com, CareerBuilder.com, TheLadders.com, Dice.com, HotJobs.com, and Job.com) and find those jobs that satisfy your passion. Then, go after those jobs.

Prisoner of War (POW)—Capture Your Dream Job

Simultaneously, *network* with all of the people who possess, know about, and desire those dream jobs. Use your network to identify unpublished job vacancies. Work your network to obtain interviews for these jobs. Capture one of those dream jobs.

Basic Training—Qualify Yourself

Additionally, simultaneously do everything you can to *prepare yourself,* your resume, and your reputation such that everyone will know that you are the best person to fill that dream job. If you have all of the tickets and all of the blocks on the application form filled, you maximize your probability of being hired for that dream job.

Green Beret—World Class

If you are *"world class"* or the best in the world at whatever is your dream job, the world will seek you out to fill that dream job. You won't need to look for and find the job of your dreams. The job will seek you out and pursue you. Also, *if you build the best thingamajig in the world, though your home may be located deep in the woods, the world will make a beaten path to your door.*

> **Uda Bomb # 2**
>
> *If you build the best thingamajig in the world, though your home may be located deep in the woods, the world will make a beaten path to your door.*

Terror Cells—Networking Is the Hottest Thing to Do

Networking is one of the hottest things to do in job searching. That is the thing to do today. Everyone thinks networking is the next best thing to sliced bread. And it is! However, do not overdo it. You only have 24 hours in a day. So, do not see or talk to every Tom, Dick, Harry, and GI Joe that crosses your path. Do

> **Uda Bomb # 3**
>
> *Networking is one of the hottest things to do in job searching.*

not attend every job fair or conference. Do not attend every professional organizational meeting or job-networking meeting. If you did all of these things to the exclusion of other necessary activities, you will be wasting a lot of your valuable time.

Susan Wilson Solovic said, "Effective networking is time-consuming, and you may think that you're too busy managing your home, family, or business to find time. But if your goal is to have success and power, you can't afford not to network. You never know when you'll meet someone who will be instrumental in helping you to achieve your goals."[3]

Insurgency—Strategic Networking with High-Value People

What you should do is strategic networking. In other words, pick high-value people with which to network. What I mean here by "high value" people are not necessarily those high-ranking executives. I mean those people who can give you a job, get you a job, or influence someone to hire you. Spend your time networking with those high-value people.

The number of networking, professional association, civic, and charitable group events held in any given week can be overwhelming. Don't drive yourself crazy trying to hit them all—be smart. Carefully select the events that you believe are the best fit for you personally and professionally.[4]

Target of Opportunity—Focus On Job Networking

Battle Stations—Career Networking vs. Job-Search Networking

If your networking is not involved with mutually helping each other to get a job, meeting people who can get you a job, or providing you information to help you obtain a job, then you are wasting your time networking. Do not mix and confuse career networking with job-search networking. *If laid off and seeking work, your primary responsibility is to find a job*. Hence, if you are networking, it should be for capturing a job. After you obtain a job, then you can continue your career-advancement networking.

---

3   Susan Wilson Solovic, "Why Networking Clubs Aren't Just for the Boys," *CareerJournal.com*. Extracted on 4/16/07 from http://www.careerjournal.com.

4   Ibid.

Cold War—Networking is a Continual Process

Networking to create solid job referrals and future contacts is a critical element of your job search. Keeping in touch with your network contacts (or nodes) must be routinely done on a regular basis ... even after you land your most important dream job.

> ## Uda Bomb # 4
>
> *If laid off and seeking work, your primary responsibility is to find a job.*

Referrals really do happen more casually than you might expect. Your college roommate's husband's friend is as likely to land you your next gig as your roommate herself—but only if she knows you're looking for a job when she hears about one.[5]

Commando—Networking for Consulting Gigs

Networking is extremely important in consulting. I initially started consulting for Hughes Aircraft Company through a good program manager friend of mine. That first gig at Hughes grew into other subsequent consulting gigs, which resulted from networking that I had established while working there.

Barbara Safani gives the following seven rules for networking success:

1. Ask for information, not a job
2. Be considerate of others' time
3. Listen first; then ask questions
4. Expand your network
5. Follow up
6. Reciprocate
7. Send a thank you letter

---

[5] Eileen P. Gunn, "Why Networking is Still the Best Way to Job Hunt," *CareerJournal.com*. Extracted on 4/16/07 from http://www.careerjournal.com.

Successful networkers show a sincere interest in their networking contacts. They're constantly developing relations, establishing their credibility, and sharing information. They follow the rules of the game where everyone has something to gain. Like the lottery, you have to be in it to win it.[6]

Clandestine Travel—The Best Route to Find Employment

What do you think is the best source to find employment? I have been looking through job magazines, the Internet, and word of mouth. I remember you saying that the Internet is probably one of the worse sources to use. I am not sure if I should be looking for an immediate opening or if I should be looking for a company that I really want to work for and go for an entry level job within that company. Right now, I guess my main focus is getting the experience that every business wants. What do you think would be the best route?

Global Information Grid (GIG)—Develop Good Nodes

I think the best source of employment is your developed "nodes" of your network. The "nodes" are your contact points. *Networking is king or queen.* Develop those nodes. I desire the best students in my classes as my nodes, which I add to my network. I obtained my consulting jobs because of networking. I captured my job at QUAL-COMM because of networking. I nailed my teaching jobs because of networking. *Networking is the best source to find employment.* So, start developing your network by developing good "nodes."

> **Uda Bomb # 5**
>
> *Networking is the best source to find employment.*

---

6   Barbara Safani, "Seven Rules for Networking Success," *TheLadders.com Weekly Executive Coach*, October 24, 2007.

Gather G-2—Do Your Due Diligence

Yes, look for about five companies that you really want to work for and do the due diligence on these companies. Gather information, develop contacts, and keep up with the companies. Yes, go for an entry-level job within those five companies. Methodically work towards that objective. Prepare occupational analysis reports (OARs) on each of those companies. Gather information from each company's website. Work to infiltrate those companies to meet and chat with employees.

War College—Professional Growth

Yes, *continue to develop your skills and experience that every business wants.* Here is the best route:

> **Uda Bomb # 6**
>
> *Continue to develop your skills and experience that every business wants.*

- *Resume.* Continue to "beef up" and polish your resume and cover letter
- *Organizations.* Join a professional organization or two in your career area of choice and place them on your resume
- *Service.* Get involved in serving on committees, run for office, and participate in meetings of these professional organizations
- *Education.* Take additional technical courses and earn certifications in your career area of choice that you can add to your resume
- *Bullets.* Continue to do great things on your internship and other jobs to develop good bullets to add to your resume
- *Meetings.* Attend conferences, seminars, workshops, and trade shows in your career area of choice
- *Papers.* Prepare papers to present at these conferences and publish in their proceedings

- *Articles.* Prepare articles to publish in these professional organizations' periodicals
- *Book.* Write a book on your career area of interest and publish it

The Complete Soldier—A Balanced Program

If you do these things, you will have a dynamite of a cover letter and resume. You will receive many calls for interviews. You will perform well in interviews and receive several offers. You will be able to negotiate the best deal you can get with every offer. You will be able to leverage one offer against another to maximize your final offer and job. You will be able to perform well on your jobs so that you will receive all the benefits that that job offers. You will be able to prepare more "beefy" resume bullets for each new job you secure. The process will continue *ad infinitum.*

Infiltration—Best Way to Break Into Any Company

The best way to break into any company is to have someone (like a mole) on the inside working to get you in. This is why networking is one of the most important weapons and strategies for seeking a good job. If it weren't for networking, I wouldn't have obtained most of my jobs. I wouldn't have been on the consulting gigs I had acquired if it weren't for networking. Therefore, take maximum advantage of networking.

> ## Uda Bomb # 7
>
> *The best way to break into any company is to have someone on the inside working to get you in. This is why networking is one of the most important weapons and strategies for seeking a good job.*

Dirty Bombs—Slobs Will Not Get the Good Jobs

Full Battle Gear—Dress Appropriately

I looked at some of the photographs that were posted on a website showing job fairs. I was totally amazed and appalled to see that most of the students that visited the booths were dressed like total slobs. If they were expecting to make a bad impression on the recruiters and really didn't want a job, then they were dressed exactly right for that job fair. If you are applying for a laborer or outside job, then you may dress like a slob. However, if you are applying for a professional job working indoors, then I suggest you dress in a more presentable manner. That's my bomb damage assessment (BDA).

Class A Uniform—Dress to Impress, Not Depress

You attend job fairs to network. When you network with a company for which you would like to work, you should dress in a manner that would impress instead of depress those manning the booth. The recruiters at these booths are usually dressed pretty well. Why? Because they are trying to impress you! So, what makes these students feel that they are in such great demand that they too don't need to dress appropriately to impress the recruiters!

Mess Dress—Better to Overdress Than Under-dress

On every job fair I had attended in the past, I dressed in a white shirt, tie, and dark suit. For a job fair held outside, perhaps you don't need to dress up to that extent. However, the guys should at least be in a dress shirt and tie if it is too hot outside to wear a coat. The women usually dress better than the men do.

> **Uda Bomb # 8**
>
> *It is better to be overdressed than under-dressed.*

However, just because the guys dress like slobs, that doesn't mean the gals should dress like slobs also. If you want a "competitive edge" over your competitors, dress appropriately for any and every occasion that you attend to network, get to know, and positively impress people. *It is better to be overdressed than under-dressed.*

GI Pack—Avoid Wearing Backpacks to Interviews

When you go to a job interview, do you wear your backpack with all of your books in them? You don't, right? So, why do I see so many students wearing backpacks to job fairs? Why don't they carry their rifles with them also and look like an insurgent? Just because some job fairs are held on campus, that doesn't excuse you from looking like a high school student. Leave your backpack in your car, store it somewhere safe, or have one of your friends not attending the job fair watch it for you while you are at the job fair.

Inspection—Avoid a Sloppy Image

If I were hiring people (and I have hired many people during my career), I wouldn't hire anyone looking like a slob. What is the reason for that? It is because they, in all probability, will perform the work on the job the same way … as slobs. Their work will be sloppy. Their office will look sloppy. They will present a sloppy image to our customers. That's why!

> ### Uda Bomb # 9
> *Slobs will not get the good jobs.*

Remember this: *Slobs will not get the good jobs.* Dress is very important. Dress appropriately to make a good impression. Do it right!

Revolution—Is There Conflict of Interest in This Situation?

A position you have been wanting with a company for a long time comes available. You hear about this job through a good friend, and the only problem is that your direct boss is his/her mom. You are very positive that if you show interest or hope of getting that job, it will happen because of your friend. Do you interview for the job?

There are two ways to interpret this question. The first way is that you are currently working for your good friend's mom in your current company, and your good friend tells you about this good job lead in another company. The second way is that this job lead in another company that your good friend tells you about is the position where his/her mom would be your new direct boss.

First Wave—The First Interpretation of the Question

Yes, by all means, interview for the job. Your good friend brought this job lead to your attention. He/she must have thought through the fact that should you be hired for this new job, you would need to quit working for his/her mom. There would be a conflict of interest only if you had approached your friend to get a job (this job) for you and if your friend was concerned that he/she would be hurting his/her mom by pulling you away from your current employment working for her.

Furthermore, it's not like you are in a critical position with your present company. If you were a vice president, member of the board of directors, chief scientist, major stockholder, or key personnel, then there might be some pause and discussions with your management before you would make any kind of move.

However, I surmise that you are not in a critical position; hence, you should explore opportunities to better yourself. Also, after you receive an offer, the way your management reacts to it will indicate your present value to the organization. If they don't care, push you out the door, or don't counter your offer, then you will have a better idea of what they think of you. Hence, it is good that you are leaving for greener pastures.

Second Wave—The Second Interpretation of the Question

By all means, yes, interview for the job. What do you think good friends and good networking nodes are for? Here is an opportune way to capture a good job. However, be sure that you can work for your good friend's mom. I am assuming that you probably already know her well. Being a good friend of someone also means that you have probably been over to his/her home quite often, have met his/her parents, and have gotten to know them well. I say, go for it!

Abu Ghraib Prison—Abusive Networking

One of the best avenues for exploring the hidden job market is networking—using your friends, acquaintances, and referrals to scope out unadvertised job opportunities. Most job seekers use some degree of networking in their campaigns. Unfortunately, some of them—inadvertently or otherwise—are abusing the networking process, which may diminish its impact for everyone.[7]

Death March—Networking Abuse

Abuse of the networking process can be as simple as contacting the same person too frequently or overstaying one's welcome at an appointment. In many cases, abuse is simply overuse that results from poor planning and inadequate self-pacing in the job search. Successful networkers pace themselves by arranging calls and meetings at an easily managed tempo.[8]

Traitor—Bad Node

I had a person call me and requested a reference letter within two days. Being the nice guy that I am, I obliged by staying up late in the evening and completing the letter. I got no thank you for it. Then, a month later, this same person calls and leaves me a voice mail messages stating that she needed another letter of reference the next day and wondered if I would do it. I ignored that voice mail message. This person was abusing me as a networking node. I could do without that person on my networking list.

---

7 William J. Morin, "The Secret to Mastering 'Non-abusive' Networking," *CareerJournal.com*. Extracted on 4/16/07 from http://www.careerjournal.com.

8 Ibid.

Gitmo—Guard Your Network

What all this finally means is this: Use your network, but use it cautiously. These contacts may be some of the most valuable you'll make in your career. Guard them jealously and treat them with care. Many people become unemployed or need to make a job change more than once in their careers. The way [you] treat networking contacts the first time around will determine not only their immediate impact on your career, but also how much they'll be available to help you in the future.[9]

Ally—Good Node

I have another friend who had asked me if I would prepare a letter of recommendation for him as he was applying to an MBA program at one of the local universities in a month from that time. I said I was glad to do it. That night, I prepared the letter and sent it to him. He was so impressed that I had done it immediately instead of taking the month of time in which he said he needed it. He profusely thanked me for it and thanked me again on several occasions after that. He has also done a lot of things for me. That is the kind of networking node I want to keep, not the other kind that take and take but never give anything in return.

Booby Traps—Networking Traps to Guard Against

Fratricide—Inept Networking

Douglas Richardson said, "Networking is still the most effective job-search and self-marketing tool, but when done ineptly, it's also the most obnoxious. Many job hunters blunder through the process, causing potential employers and contacts to feel misused and manipulated."[10]

---

[9] Ibid.

[10] Douglas B. Richardson, "Savvy Job Hunters Learn to Network Nicely," *CareerJournal.com*. Extracted on 4/16/07 from http://www.careerjournal.com.

Meal, Ready to Eat (MRE)—Canned Networking Technique

Networking is being packaged as a canned, impersonal, and manipulative technique. As a result, a lot of bad networking occurs. Many networking contacts are feeling used and abused, and the abusers are poisoning the well for others. Regardless of what the process is called, humans will always help each other unless their efforts are demeaned and unreciprocated. Job seekers who ignore this truth deserve the hostility they receive.[11]

---

[11] Ibid.

Chapter 2
Training Camp—Preparation

*E*ven *if it doesn't come naturally, networking is an art that can be learned. You don't have to be inherently gregarious and outgoing. Just have a genuine curiosity and interest in others. The result can be personally and professionally rewarding.*[12]

Chuck Hester, APR

Fundamentalism—What is Networking?

Networking is defined as establishing contacts, exchanging information, and/or developing relationships with others in informal networks for the purpose of obtaining employment or a job, getting a date, or furthering one's career. The key to networking is to be a good node/reference and to cultivate good nodes/references in informal networks.

Terminology—Definition of Networking Terms

What is the difference between "reference" and "network"? Also, what is a "network node"? A "reference" is a *person* who provides either you or someone else (in your behalf) with a letter or phone response (i.e., verification/validation information) of you and your background, capabilities, and desirability. A "reference" is also the *material/information* that a "reference or referrer" gives about you to others. Hence, a "reference" may be

---

[12] Chuck Hester, "Hello, My Name is...: Networking is an Art That Can Be (Painlessly) Learned." *Public Relations Tactics*, April 2007, p. 21.

both the *person* providing the reference information and the *material/information* itself that is provided.

A "network" is the *list* of names/contact coordinates of your "references." A "network node" is *a specific person* on your network list. Hence, a "network node or networking node" is a specific "reference" or person on your "network" list of references.

Furthermore, a "network" also is the combination of all of your "network nodes" located throughout the country. For example, if you placed a huge map of the United States on your wall, stuck a pin in every location of each of your networking nodes, and drew lines from each of your networking nodes to the pin representing you and your location, you would see the entire network of your "contacts." Additionally, if you were to draw connecting lines between and among whichever networking nodes that know each other, you would have a complete picture that truly represents your complete personal "network," which may look like a spider's web, fish net, or cell structure. Hence, networking can variously be called:

- Meshing (like a wire-mesh fence)
- Netting (like a fish net or hair net)
- Matrixing (like an Excel chart of rows and columns)
- Webbing (like a spider's web)
- Celling (like a cell phone network)
- Combing (like a honeycomb network).

Battle Array—Types of Networking

There are several types of networking:

- *Job or Employment Networking*—network to land a new job
- *Career Networking*—after you land a job, then career networking follows to advance your career
- *Social Networking*—this is a lonely hearts club or networking for dates and/or a future mate

Rest and Recuperation (R&R)—Social Networking

Peter Weddle asks, "Networking is one of the best strategies for finding a new or better job. Right? Right. And, social networking clearly involves networking. Right? Right. So, social networking is the new and improved way to land the job of your dreams. Right? Wrong."[13]

It's hard to miss the buzz about social networking. The media has been all agog over the rapid rise of such sites as MySpace. They attract millions of visitors every month, providing lots of opportunity for individual interaction and relationship building. While this activity is indeed networking, the most important aspect of its description is the adjective that defines it—social. That may be a ton of fun, but it's unlikely to get you hired.[14]

In the past, I've used the term "e-networking" to describe electronic or online networking. But with the rise of the social networking, I've redefined it as "employment networking." E-networking—employment networking—is unlike its very social cousin in three important ways:

- It has a different purpose.
- It is done in a different way.
- It takes place on different web sites.[15]

Conspirator—Be a Good Networking Node

Here is what one of my previous students wrote to me:

Hi Bob: Here is my version of a recommendation letter. Hope you like it. Thank you.

---

13 Peter D. Weddle, "Will Social Networking Get You a Job?," *Yahoo! HotJobs.* Extracted on 4/16/07 from http://hotjobs.yahoo.com.

14 Ibid.

15 Ibid.

Thank you for the rough draft. I have put my "English" on it and am sending my draft to you for your review. Please suggest any changes you would like me to make to it. After you approve it, I will print up copies on good paper, sign them, and send them to you. Bob Uda

The student replied again with the following:

Hi Bob: Thank you so much. I love it. With this letter, I know I will get a job. Thank you and if you ever need anything, please ask.

I'm glad you like the letter of recommendation I prepared for you.

Regarding your comment on "Thank you and if you ever need anything, please ask," please understand that good networking nodes usually don't need to be asked, unless it is a returned favor "in kind." Therefore, as good networking nodes, we should always be on the lookout to return favors to our fellow nodes without them needing to ask for anything in return.

For example, Dave Blackledge agrees to speak to my SSM 445 class, and I make sure that we have a Certificate of Appreciation and CSUSM coffee mug to present to him after his speech. I also send him a thank you email the day after the speech. He tries to get me a consulting assignment with his company, as I submitted him and his company for the Award for Outstanding Service Learning Community Partner with the CSUSM Office of Community Service Learning (OCSL). He did not ask for any of these favors.

Additionally, Dave gives me a lead to a job opening for which I had interviewed, and he also offers to serve as a reference for me. I didn't ask him for these favors. He also "greased the skids" for me with the hiring manager, who is a good friend of his. I didn't ask for this. During the interview, I also praised Dave to this hiring manager. Furthermore, I automatically am working to get Dave an adjunct faculty position because he wants to teach part time. He didn't ask me to do these things. Do you get the picture of what it takes to be a good networking node?

Unfortunately, I don't think some students really understand what comprises a good networking node. If they did, they wouldn't ask me to do the numerous things they've asked me to do for them, and then do absolutely nothing in return. Furthermore, they keep asking and asking and asking but never reciprocating. People who will not automatically dream up things to do in return should not ask for anything from anyone! Being a good networking node is simple as that.

Being a good networking node requires "receiving" and subsequent "giving." It is a two-way affair. It is not a one-way affair as many students think. I really believe that they do not understand the concerted effort it requires to be a good networking node. If people will not uphold their side of the networking bargain, then I don't want them as a networking node. It is as simple as that!

Only about five or six students in each of my classes ever qualify to be good networking nodes because they learn and understand the obligation of the unspoken reciprocity required whenever they receive help. These people will go far in their careers and in life in general. I want to keep tabs of these people throughout their careers.

Most people do not ever learn how to be good networking nodes because, basically, they are selfish and only want to receive but never ever think of giving back anything. The only reciprocity they think of and do is to screw you. What kind of networking node does that make them? With friends like that, who needs enemies!

> ## Uda Bomb #10
>
> *Learn what a "true" networking node is and practice the obligations and reciprocity involved. In legal terms, we call it "quid pro quo," which means "something for something" or "the giving of one valuable thing for another."*

So, *learn what a "true" networking node is and practice the obligations and reciprocity involved. In legal terms, we call it quid pro quo, which means "something for something" or "the giving of one valuable thing for another."* Only then will people help you out as you network with them. Do you get the picture?

Harvey Mackay said, "The more you exercise your networking muscles, the stronger they'll get—and the easier networking becomes."[16]

If you don't want to mutually help anyone, then don't ask anyone for anything. You will not receive anything of significance in all of your future jobs. Additionally, don't expect anything of significance in your career either. On the other hand, *be a good networking node, and you will go far in life!*

Netwar—Networking Methods

What methods can be used for networking? Some of the methods that can be used to network and communicate are as follows:

- Talking face-to-face in meetings and/or interviews

- Talking by telephone one-on-one and by conference call

- Writing and sending letters/memos/cards by snail mail

- Preparing, sending, and receiving faxes

- Writing, sending, and receiving email through the Internet

- Talking through teleconferencing, videoconferencing, and web cameras

> ## Uda Bomb #11
>
> *Be a good networking node, and you will go far in life!*

---

16 Harvey Mackay, "Some Winning Strategies for Reluctant Networkers," *CareerJournal.com*. Extracted on 4/16/07 from http://www.careerjournal.com.

- Communicating through text messages on Palm Pilots and BlackBerries
- Communicating through chat rooms, web logs (blogs), and instant messaging

Campaign—Networking Lists

I started working on my networking list and have a couple of questions. Is it bad that three of my networking buddies are from where I am currently working (they are at different locations but still in the same company)? Furthermore, do you have any examples? I do not really like my format and was wondering if any others look better than mine. How detailed should it be as related to how I think they will help me in the future?

Targeting—Select Only Quality Nodes

No, it is not bad that three of your networking buddies are from where you work. The most important criterion is whether your networking nodes (i.e., buddies) are quality nodes. In other words, you can effectively communicate with and maintain throughout your career only a limited number of networking nodes. Hence, it is very important that your nodes are quality nodes … those you help and vice versa.

Training—Cultivate Your Quality Nodes

You can have an endless list of networking buddies/nodes, but you will want to cultivate and maintain only about 10 of them as quality nodes throughout your career and lifetime. These nodes are the people whom you trust implicitly, meet with periodically, keep in touch with by phone/email throughout your career,

> ## Uda Bomb # 12
>
> *If networking is only a one-way affair, it is for naught. It must be a mutually beneficial relationship.*

and mutually depend on helping with letters of reference and job references.

Coalition Forces—A Mutually Beneficial Relationship

Make your list as detailed as necessary for it to be effective in helping you in the future. Remember this: *If networking is only a one-way affair, it is for naught. It must be a mutually beneficial relationship*. Remember that.

Battlefield—Build a Network

Build a network of people that provide mutual help. This is the most productive use of your time. However, there is a method to this madness. You must network smartly with intelligence. Do not network for the sake of networking, but network for positive, constructive results. If you do not achieve good results, you are not networking effectively.

> **Uda Bomb # 13**
>
> *Build a network of people that provide mutual help.*

Build a network and achieve the following:

- Build a network of people that provide mutual help
- Develop a wide network of friends and collaborators
- Develop a fine-tuned network of mutual, complementary job-searching peers and helpers
- Attend networking meetings and events
- Cultivate good job references through your network
- Join ClubNet (Job Club) and participate in professional networking
- Network through the deans of your college
- Network with friends of a friend

Ambush—Networking at Relevant Places and Events

Safe Houses—Examples of Places to Network

Let us look at what could be considered as relevant networking places and events. These are some examples of places and events where you can network with relevant people:

- Job networking meetings or gatherings
- Career or job classes, courses, and seminars
- Technical conventions
- Trade shows
- Professional organizational meetings
- Job or career shows and fairs
- Career or job centers
- Company open houses with potential work for you
- Small Business Administration (SBA) events

Cells—Networking Groups and Meetings

Attend professional networking groups and professional society chapter meetings. These groups and meetings provide a wealth of resources and often lead to credible contacts and leads for job opportunities. Participating in these networking groups raises your awareness on industrial issues and job-search challenges. Because you are involved with peers with similar career directions, they may offer volunteer opportunities that can be specifically related to your career direction.

Brigades—Structured-networking Groups

We keep hearing that the best way to find an executive job is through networking. But not everyone knows how to network effectively or has good contacts to mine. This may explain the allure of structured-networking groups — organizations that schedule meetings and other opportunities for members to connect and share job leads with the help of facilitators.[17]

Battles—Structured Networking Events

Barbara Mende showed a sampling of national and regional organizations offering structured networking events as follows:

- ExecuNet
- The Five O'Clock Club
- The Financial Executives Networking Group
- Technology Executives Networking Group
- Forty Plus
- Professional Area Network for Women in Technology[18]

These get-togethers range from informal meetings to formal programs with prescribed reading or coursework. The groups offering them may be for-profit, not-for-profit, or state-sponsored. Defined by profession, income level, geography, demographic, or some combination of these factors, they seek to make job hunters comfortable with networking.[19]

Defense Budget—Membership Fees

Networking organizations may offer other assistance as well and charge higher membership fees to provide it. However, the group-networking events tend to be affordable—in the $30 to $45 range—and their organizers stress that everyone participates.[20]

---

[17] Barbara Mende, "Structured Groups Can Help if You Missed Networking 101," *CareerJournal.com*. Extracted on 4/16/07 from http://www.careerjournal.com.

[18] Barbara Mende, "A Guide to Finding Structured-Networking Groups," *CareerJournal.com*. Extracted on 4/16/07 from http://www.careerjournal.com.

[19] Barbara Mende, "Structured Groups Can Help if You Missed Networking 101," *CareerJournal.com*. Extracted on 4/16/07 from http://www.careerjournal.com.

[20] Ibid.

Maneuvers — Preparation for Networking Event

Be prepared to be sized up when you step into the networking scene. Here's a quick list to help you stand up to the scrutiny:

- Dress appropriate to the venue. If the event is at a person's home, a three-piece suit is probably not required.
- Practice your handshake. Firm—not abusive.
- Pop a breath mint—or two.
- Don't be overbearing. As strange as it seems, some people attend these events to unwind. The strong sell won't work.
- Take plenty of business cards.[21]

Confrontation — Strike a Happy Balance

However, do not overdo networking at these places and events. You have many other important activities to spend your valuable time doing in your 24-hour day. These activities include:

- Polishing and sending out your resume
- Telephoning your contact list
- Taking free computer classes at the career center
- Researching on job websites
- Working on professional certifications
- Preparing and presenting papers at conventions
- Writing and publishing a book

So, strike a good, happy balance.

---

21 Christopher Jones, "Six Degrees of Employment," *Yahoo! HotJobs*. Extracted on 4/16/07 from http://hotjobs.yahoo.com.

Containment—Lesser Productive Places and Events

Retreat—Examples of Places Not to Waste Your Time Networking

There are other places and events that networking can be done, but they generally are not as productive as those mentioned above because they are not specifically related to job searching, companies with which you could work, or where work-related topics are discussed. Examples of some of these lesser productive places and events include the following:

- Church
- Grocery store, drug store, and other stores
- Barber shop
- Walking on the street/sidewalks
- While in a taxi or cab
- Attending a non-job-related social function
- Movie theater
- Sporting event
- Restaurants
- Visiting companies that are not in your career field
- Gas stations

Target Selection—Be Choosy

By a fluke, you could chance-meet someone at these places and events. However, the amount of time spent networking at these places/events will not be as productive as the time spent at the places/events mentioned on page 25. Therefore, be choosy in selecting the places and events at which you spend your time networking.

Perri Capell said, "If you're doing it right, networking isn't something that takes lots of extra time in your life. It easily blends into your life and your approach to life."[22]

---

[22] Perri Capell, "Finding Time: Blending Networking into Your Life," *CareerJournal.com*. Extracted on 4/16/07 from http://www.careerjournal.com.

G-2—Tips on Networking

If you want a new position, start networking now. Marshall Loeb gave these tips on how to get the most out of networking:

- Know what you're looking for.
- Be assertive.
- Curb the desperation and start listening.
- Your most valuable tools include an up-to-date resume, business cards, and follow-up phone call or email.
- Stick with it.[23]

---

23 Marshall Loeb, "If You Want a New Position, Start Networking Now," *Marketwatch*, *CareerJournal.com*. Extracted on 4/16/07 from http://www.careerjournal.com.

Chapter 3

Hand-to-Hand Combat—Performance

W hatever the approach, the bottom line is that we all need to network. By doing so, you'll meet people and exchange information
that will help you do your job more efficiently. By pursuing any
of the many available options, you will build relationships that enrich your life,
broaden your horizons, and enhance your career.[24]

Jack H. Dobson Jr., CSP
President, American Society of Safety Engineers

Walkie-talkie—Phone Calling

Evasive Measures—Avoid Cold Calling

When I was laid off once before, I remember spending hours and hours on
the telephone at the career center cold
calling everyone I knew, company after
company. You know? It was a grand waste
of time. I learned that the hard way.

Our job consultant told us that networking was the best thing to do and to
call everyone on our contact list. Well, I
did just that, and it was a huge waste of
my valuable time. *Telephoning for the
sake of telephoning is not very productive.*

> ## Uda Bomb # 14
>
> *Do strategic
> phoning, not
> telemarketing.
> People hate
> telemarketing.*

---

[24] Jack H. Dobson, Jr., "The Value of Networking." *Professional Safety*, August 2005, p. 8.
www.asse.org.

Strategy—Strategic Phoning vs. Telemarketing

Instead, find those individuals who really could provide you with good leads, advice, and help. Those are the ones with which you want to spend your time on the phone. *Do strategic phoning, not telemarketing. People hate telemarketing.*

Pinned Down—Don't Waste Time Chit-chatting

Make your phone calls work for you. You have more important things to do than just to "shoot the bull" with friends and relatives across the country. Do you realize that some people actually do that? Because they can use the career center phones for free, they call all of their friends and relatives throughout the country just to chitchat. What a waste of time ... not to mention taxpayers' money!

Sniper Targeting—Make Your Calls Count

Selective Targeting—Be Judicious in Your Calling

Every person is predominantly either a talker or a writer. If orally oriented, you would probably prefer to network face-to-face in person or by phone instead of by email. Making phone calls is good, but just making phone calls for the sake of making phone calls is not good. Cold calling is a waste of time. *We must focus on making calls to the right people in the right places at the right time.*

Perri Capell said, "Perhaps it's not just lack of time that's holding you back, but lack of confidence. It's unnerving to make calls when you doubt the person you're about to contact wants to hear from you. But when that nice email comes back, the anxiety melts away. Take some time and try it."[25]

> ### Uda Bomb # 15
>
> *We must focus on making calls to the right people in the right places at the right time.*

---

[25]   Perri Capell, "Finding Time: Blending Networking into Your Life," *CareerJournal.com.* Extracted on 4/16/07 from http://www.careerjournal.com.

Wild-goose Chase—Phone Tag

Since the advent of voice mail, one of the real drawbacks of using the telephone is that people will only return calls to callers with whom they want to speak. The pervasive telemarketing industry has soured many people in returning calls to names of people and/or phone numbers they do not readily recognize. Additionally, people are so busy these days that it is extremely difficult to get them to answer the phone the moment you call. You could play "phone tag" for days on end, which wastes a lot of your valuable time.

Plan of Attack—Develop a Phoning List

Hence, if you prefer to network by phone, develop a list of names, titles, companies, and phone numbers of the right selection of people to call. Make at least 10 to 15 calls per day. From these calls, you may generate 1 to 2 interviews for an opportunity. If you do not make 10-15 calls a day, you will not build up a head of steam and keep the momentum going.

Mop Up—Follow Up

Another point in phone networking is to:

(1) Make a call

(2) Follow it with an email

(3) Follow the email with a follow-up call

If you receive no response, go on to the next contact. In your phone conversation, do not come across as being desperate.

> **Uda Bomb # 16**
>
> *There is a fine line between being persistent and being a pest.*

Hot Pursuit—Persistent vs. Pest

Refrain from making repeated calls or queries to someone who neither returns your calls nor responds to your emails. In other words, do not be a pest. *There is a fine line between being persistent and being a pest.* You do not want to be a pest, particularly if the person you are calling is actively avoiding you. If he does not want to speak with you, chances are he will not hire you. So, why waste your time?

Buddy System—Mentor and Mentoring

It is extremely important for you to recruit a good mentor. You need someone who is objective and who will give you frank, no-holds-barred advice and suggestions for improvement. This mentor can look at your resume and give you pointers for improvement. This mentor can give you ideas on how to interview effectively. This mentor can validate your job-search strategies, tactics, and assumptions. Finally, this mentor can help you to gain a broader perspective in your job search.

Recruitment—Select a Good Mentor

Not anyone can serve effectively as a mentor. Select someone who is conducting a successful job search or someone who recently had completed a successful job search. This mentor must be well versed in today's job market. Your job search coach from your outplacement firm is not necessarily a good mentoring candidate. That job search coach probably has not searched for a job in years and, hence, is dated in his or her knowledge of the strategies that work in this present-day job-searching environment.

> ## Uda Bomb # 17
>
> *It is extremely important for you to recruit a good mentor.*

Buddy—Mutual Mentoring

A good friend and I served each other as mutual mentors. There was no holding back in commenting on the resume and other aspects of the job search. This friend analyzed a previous book I had written. His comments contributed tremendously to improving the contents of that book. I am grateful for his contributions.

Body Armor—Thick Skin Required

You must have a thick skin if you are to learn anything from your mentor. You must not take anything personally as a put down. Look for the message. I was frank with a person when I commented on his resume (he had asked me to comment on his resume). He took offense at my "cutting to the chase." It was too bad for him. He did not learn much from receiving redlines on his resume. It was a

> **Uda Bomb # 18**
>
> *You must have a thick skin if you are to learn anything from your mentor.*

waste of my time. Do not be like that. If you are overly sensitive, do not recruit a mentor. You do not need one, and the potential mentor does not need you either.

Deterrence—Networking with Classmates

You had mention that we should network with our classmates, right? However, if we do network with our classmates, but we don't hangout or socialize much, what makes me think they will help me hook up with a job while they probably have friends that are close to them who might also need a job?

Networking with your classmates is a good thing. For one thing, you all are looking for jobs around the same time-period. As you search for jobs, say on the Internet, you may stumble upon job ads that would fit well your other classmates. You can then forward those job leads to them.

Coordinated Attack—Two-way Street

Now, networking is a two-way street. As you help others, they too will find job leads in their search that may match your background better. If they have received job leads from you, they will feel obligated to return the favor by sending you those job leads that would benefit you. Hence, instead of only yourself searching for suitable job ads, you may have up to 46 other students in your class providing you with suitable job leads. How does that increase your productivity? Tremendously!

Booby Trap—Not a One-way Street

Remember this: *Networking is not a "one-way street."* Those who are good at networking always help each other in their network. Hence, networking is a "two-way street." Never do I take help from anyone without always thinking how I would return the favor. You must take the same approach if others will ever consider you as a good networking "node." There is nothing worse than the person who takes and takes and takes but never gives anything back in return.

> **Uda Bomb # 19**
>
> *Networking is not a "one-way street."*

Teamwork—Good Networking

Christopher Michel, CEO of Military.com, said, "*Good networking is not a one-time activity; it is about staying in touch, providing value to your contacts, and giving back. The sincerity of your relationships matter—no one wants to hear from you only when you need something. If you start networking in conjunction with your job search, you already are behind the power curve. The best networkers do not see networking as a short cut to a job—they thrive on connecting with people, helping others, and staying in touch throughout their lives.*"[26]

An Army of 1—Selfishness

In today's world, selfishness is rampant. Instead of dishing out good to others, many people dish out nothing but negativism, screw each other,

---

[26] Christopher Michel, "Make Networking Work for You," Military.com, http://www.military.com, January 6, 2004.

and stab each other in the back. I would never want as one of my networking nodes a person who has continually worked to screw me, and we have many of those around us … even students! I would never consider these people as part of my networking nodes and would never help them to get ahead.

Traitors—Avoid Backstabbers as You Would the Plague

For example, here is a course critique that one of my former students wrote about me in his critique: "*This man obviously is not a teacher, and I feel cheated out of an opportunity that may have proven otherwise useful. He is a shameless self-promoter and charlatan, and it showed on a daily basis. Shame on whoever allowed this to happen.*"

See what I mean? Would you like this person as one of your networking nodes? Never in a million years! Do not use people like this as references. You are doomed to failure if you do. Avoid backstabbers as you would the plague. Just think, someone today has this person working for him or her.

Pin-point Targeting—Select Your Networking Nodes Wisely

So, think about whom you can help. You may be surprised that some of your nodes will give back to you much more than you will have ever given to them. These people are the ones who you would want to cultivate as important nodes in your network.

> # Uda Bomb # 20
> *Remember, fellow networking student nodes started great companies.*

Shipmates—Great Companies Started with Classmate Nodes

Remember, fellow networking student nodes started great companies. For example, college classmates started companies such as Hewlett-Packard and Apple Computer. Therefore, do not underestimate the potential of your fellow classmates as future business partners.

Intimidation—Networking and Awkward Silence

My question is regarding networking. I am getting better at introducing myself to people I want to meet at events; however, after introductions and a brief chat, there always seems to be an awkward silence. What are some good closing/departure lines for ending a conversation?

Yes, never let the conversation get to a point of an awkward silence. As soon as you complete with what you need to say after a brief conversation, just say, "It was nice meeting you, and I hope to see you again." Shake hands, smile, and depart. Just make it a smooth transition.

Remember this: When a conversation comes to an awkward silence, I assure you, both parties feel uncomfortable. I kid you not! Hence, do not let your conversation get to that point. Close and depart at the peak of the upswing, not at the bottom of the downswing. Got it?

Suicide Bombing—Fallacy: "Network with everybody and anybody."

You can waste more of your valuable time following this bad advice. People who spend all of their time making call after call on the phone, talking to every Tom, Dick, Harry, and GI Joe that cross their path, and attending every professional meeting, job-related public event, and job fair are wasting their valuable time.

Judy Rosemarin wrote, "Networking doesn't mean making thousands of contacts. Instead, write provocative letters introducing yourself, then arrange ways to discuss mutually interesting subjects with a few key people. If you view your job search as a personal research project on a compelling subject—your own future—you'll find it easier to collect critical information and ideas."[27]

---

[27]   Judy Rosemarin, "Networking Strategies for Shy Professionals," *CareerJournal.com.* Extracted on 4/16/07 from http://www.careerjournal.com.

Sunni Triangle—Job-search Network Triangle

As the broader base of your job-search network triangle increases, the number of people you need to speak with to reach the right decision makers increases. Hence, the time it takes to reach the key decision makers increases.

Zero Hour—Not Enough Hours in the Day; Need to Be Judicious

You do not have enough hours in the day to talk with everyone, particularly if you also have to spend time searching job sites on the Internet, preparing and sending out resumes, attending job fairs, attending seminars/computer classes, making job-search phone calls, and reading job-search articles. This is why it is not such a good idea to speak with every neighbor, postal delivery person, milkman, yardman, church member, door-to-door solicitor, friend, relative, former employees, classmates, and strangers in the marketplace. They are all well intentioned but not connected to the apex of your job-search network triangle. Hence, *you need to be judicious on whom you talk to in your networking activities.*

Friendly Fire Freak Accident—A Fluke

One job expert related the story of the man who got a vice-presidential position because he had a chance conversation with his garbage man, whose next-door neighbor had an acquaintance that happened to be in the market for a vice-president. If you talked to a million garbage men, do you think acquiring a vice president's job would repeat itself? No, not likely. It was a fluke!

Uda Bomb # 21

You need to be judicious on whom you talk to in your networking activities.

Extremist—One Data Point Does Not a Trend Make

It was a once-in-a-million probability of occurrence. It is a statistical out-lier. By using a single data point to indicate that you can obtain jobs by talking to everybody (even your garbage man), this job expert gives bad advice by diverting you from your primary job-search activities. Where's the trend line!

You would be more productive and effective talking to people in your industry that know of job openings in their companies. This approach enhances your focus and effectiveness and further increases your odds of finding the job you are seeking. A side benefit is that you can validate your value, experience, and credentials with those in the know within the indus-try of today's job market.

Counterintelligence—How Can I Obtain Hard-to-Find Information?

How can I find out a company's resignation rate and find employees who they have fired? I may be wrong, but isn't a lot of this information unobtainable to the public or anyone not on part of the management team? How else can I obtain this informa-tion? Is there a website to which I can go to get hard-to-find information?

INTEL—Open Sources

> **Uda Bomb # 22**
>
> *Where there is a will, there is a way.*

I just made a list of the kinds of sources and methods for acquiring intelli-gence or information that would help you reach a truer understanding of the corporate culture of a company. As you point out, some information may appear to be unobtainable. However, *where there is a will, there is way.* Of course, readily available information is easy to obtain from the follow-ing open sources:

- Library, databases, info banks, and repositories
- Internet (company websites, stock market websites, web-news sites, and search engines)
- Articles in newspapers, magazines, journals, and other publications
- News reports (radio, television, and Internet)
- Company brochures, fliers, reports, and collateral
- Annual reports, 10K reports, and Dun & Bradstreet reports
- Conferences, seminars, workshops, conventions, trade shows, and meetings
- Industry sources of reference materials
- Career centers
- Your network of friends
- Any other open literature or sources

HUMINT—Other Open Sources

Now, the next level of information is from knowledgeable sources including the following:

- Knowledgeable people in the industry (headhunters, recruiters, employment agencies, consultants, researchers, and career coaches)
- Current company employees that you know (close friends in the company, someone you meet casually, and cold-called employees)
- Disgruntled current company employees [BEST SOURCES]
- Former employees (those who quit, got fired, laid off, etc.) [BEST SOURCES]
- People working in Human Resources, Finance, Security, and Administration

Espionage—Clandestine Sources

After that, you need to go to clandestine sources such as:

- Corporate spies, espionage agents, moles, detectives, and paid inside sources
- If you have the money to give away, you can find out almost anything you need about anyone or any company
- These people can:
  o Take clandestine photographs
  o Intercept emails
  o Dive for confidential information inadvertently thrown away in trash bins
  o Pay informers, squealers, snitches, traitors, and turncoats for confidential information
  o Perform wiretaps
  o Blackmail compromised people

Bugs—Grapevine

As far as salaries are concerned, I'm usually able to determine what anyone makes. Just by listening to the "grapevine," you can find out many personal things about people. There are other sources, means, and methods for gathering intelligence.

Sensors—Use Your Five Senses

To find out about resignation rates, you probably don't need to go beyond the first two sets of bullets above. To find out about fired employees, just keep your eyes and ears open. You can read, see, or hear about it in the media. Use your network. Keep your eyes and ears open. Take notes. Save articles from publications and periodicals.

> ### Uda Bomb #23
>
> *It's not what you know that counts. It's not who you know that counts. But what really counts is what you know of who you know.*

Improvise—Will and Way

As I said once before, "Where there is a will, there is a way" to find out anything and everything you want to know and use. ***Remember this:*** It's not *what* you know that counts. It's not even *who* you know that counts. But what really counts is *what you know of who you know.*

Chapter 4

Low-Intensity Conflict—Endurance

*I*n 1967, Harvard University social psychologist Stanley Milgram tested the theory when he sent 300 letters to randomly selected people in Nebraska and asked them to use their personal contacts to reach an individual they did not know in Boston. In all, 60 senders contacted the Boston individual through other people, leading Milgram to surmise that the average number of steps separating individuals in the United States is six. That led to the popular phrase "six degrees of separation." This six degrees of separation is analogous to the "six degrees of networking," which uses the so-called "small world theory."[28]

Abridged excerpt from Boston.com

Jihad—Career Networking

Who do I need to know and how do I learn to interact with others so that I am trusted and respected?

Search and Rescue—People to Get to Know

Of course, the natural ones that you would like to know are those who could help you in your career. These people include the following:

- The president
- Vice presidents
- Directors

---

28 Abridged excerpt from Boston.com, which appeared in "Six Degrees of Networking," *The Career News*, Vol. 5, Issue 22, June 6, 2005.

- Managers
- Those who are on the way to the top, i.e., fast trackers
- Those who may not have a big title but who wield much power
- Those who are real experts in a subject matter or two
- Those who are natural leaders
- Those who have all of the answers
- Friendly folks
- Key customer personnel
- Key supplier personnel
- Competitors

Joint Chiefs of Staff—Very Important People to Know

Others I like to get to know well are the receptionists in the lobby, secretaries (These days, they are called administrative assistants and executive assistants.), janitors/custodians, cafeteria workers, guards, librarians, and factory workers. You will be surprised how much these people can and will help you. If you get to know them well, they will speak well of you.

Triumph—Real-life Example

As an example, I bought lunch at a food stand outside of our work facility. This young girl from Korea worked behind the counter taking money and giving change as we purchased the food from her stand. One day, I got into a good conversation with her because my second son had served a two-year mission for our church in Korea. I had also learned a couple of greeting and farewell words in Korean. Getting into this conversation with her about my son's time in Korea and greeting/saying farewell to her in Korean had impressed her.

Well, a day thereafter, a friend came by to visit me at work on some business matters. Before he came into our facility, however, he had stopped at the food stand to buy something to munch on. This young Korean girl asked him who he was visiting at the facility. He said, "Bob Uda," to which she started raving to him about me. All this resulted from my taking about 10 minutes of my time one day talking with her and subsequently talking further with her every time I bought lunch at that stand.

My friend was so impressed that she had raved about me that he had mentioned that incident to me on more than one occasion and had told others about that incident. So, you never know how a little time and conversation can impress someone so much that they will rave about you to everyone they meet. Furthermore, the good impression snowballs to others. It is amazing how just a little kindness and friendliness can reap so much payback. It is worth spending a little time with people sharing your conversation with them.

Jihadists—You Can't Please Everybody

Remember, not everyone you meet will automatically like you. *To some people, you can do no wrong. To others, you can do no right.* Sometimes some people will have a predisposition about you. Either they had heard something negative about you from someone who dislikes you, or they may just be naturally nasty people. They may be prejudiced. They may be bigoted. They may dislike your looks. They may dislike you because of your religion, your political affiliation, or your national origin. Don't let that bother you.

> **Uda Bomb #24**
>
> *To some people, you can do no wrong. To others, you can do no right.*

Commander-in-Chief—Will Rogers

For every person with a negative disposition towards you, there are at least 10 people who will naturally like you because they subscribe to the attitude of America's 20th Century cowboy philosopher and humorist Will Rogers of Oklahoma who said, "*I never met a man I didn't like.*"

Tit for Tat—You Get What You Give

That's how I look at people. They all start out at 100 percent. And, if they so choose, they will work their way down the percent scale by saying or doing nasty things about or to me. *Be careful of how you treat people on the way up the promotion ladder, because some day you will meet them again when you are on the way down.* If you stepped all over them while you were on the way up, they may step all over you when you are on your way down. You get what you give. If you give out warm fuzzies, you will receive warm fuzzies. If you give out cold stares, you will receive cold stares. You get what you give.

> ## Uda Bomb #25
>
> *I never met a man I didn't like.*
>
> **Will Rogers**
> **Oklahoma Humorist**

Winning the Hearts and Minds—Gaining Trust and Respect

Do you want to be trusted and respected? Treat others with trust and respect. There is no better way to earn trust and respect than to give trust and respect to others. Remember the Golden Rule: *Do unto others as you would have them do unto you.* Or more simply, "*Treat others as you want to be treated.*" That's that best way to gain trust and respect from others.

Prolonged Warfare—Networking Should Be a Lifelong Activity

MBTI—Extroverts vs. Introverts

Of all of the career development activities you are involved in, networking should be your top priority. *Networking should be a lifelong activity.* Networking is somewhat easier for extroverts than it is for introverts. Extroverts usually like to talk and to socialize. Introverts like to write or listen and would

> ## Uda Bomb #26
>
> *Networking should be a lifelong activity.*

rather be alone than to talk and socialize with others. These are the reasons why networking comes more naturally to extroverts than to introverts.

Unfortunately for introverted people, it's getting more and more difficult to succeed professionally without developing a broad range of connections to other people. There simply is no such thing as a job or career field in which you can be rewarded entirely for what you know and how well you do your work. You not only have to do your job well but also make sure that others know you're doing your job well.[29]

Visibility is key. This can be trying for introverts who would rather focus on their work than on their relationships at work. And it can be downright painful for shy types who cringe at the thought of self-promotion. There's good news and bad news for introverted or shy professionals. The bad news is that networking as a means of career survival is here to stay. The good news is that networking is definitely a skill that can be learned.[30]

Judy Rosemarin suggested developing less-threatening networking techniques such as the following:

- Discard Incorrect Notions
- Learn About Yourself
- Become a Good Listener
- Connect to Your Passion
- Volunteer to Help Others
- Use Good Body Language[31]

Military Occupational Specialty (MOS)—What is Your MBTI?

I am an introvert (my Myers-Briggs Type Indicator is an INTJ) personality type. This personality type is characterized by the following indicators:

---

[29] L. Michelle Tullier, "Networking Tips for Shy Job Seekers," *CareerJournal.com*. Extracted on 4/16/07 from http://www.careerjournal.com.

[30] Ibid.

[31] Judy Rosemarin, "Networking Strategies for Shy Professionals," *CareerJournal.com*. Extracted on 4/16/07 from http://www.careerjournal.com.

- *A mastermind*—Yes, I like to dream up the grand strategy of things.

- *Contingency planning*—I always think of all of the things that can go wrong and what needs to be done to assure that there is a way out.

- *Judicious/decisive*—I make decisions quickly and never look backwards whether the decisions are right or wrong.

- *Supreme pragmatist*—Yes, being the practical person that I am, I even wrote and published a book titled *Philosophical Pragmatism: Common Sense Philosophy for the Average Person*.

- *Goal-directed actions*—Throughout life, I have always set written goals for myself, established plans for achieving those goals, and worked towards achieving those goals.

- *Open-minded*—I have always been willing to listen and consider other people's suggestions and, when determined to be good, implement them.

- *Natural brainstormer*—This has always been my *modus operandi*, which is to think of all of the possible alternatives and finding the best ways to do things.

Coercion—Introverts Need to Force Themselves to Network

Consequently, I have found it a difficult task in networking throughout my life. However, I do understand the importance of networking to career success. Hence, I have forced myself to network. It was very difficult at the beginning. However, as the years went by, I found it to be easier and easier to network.

Vulnerabilities—Shortcomings of the Introvert

As an introverted personality, I do not like to carry on endless conversations. I would rather listen than talk. I would rather write than speak. I would rather be by myself and think rather than be in

> **Uda Bomb #27**
>
> *When I was at the top of the organization, I never found it lonely up there.*

a social setting. I am happy to be alone. *When I was at the top of the organization, I never found it lonely up there.* I would rather be on the computer than on the telephone. My telephone conversations are never longer than a minute in duration.

Force Multiplier—Spouse an Extrovert

Fortunately, I married an extrovert, which helped strengthen my shortcomings in this area. Karen, my wife, must have the television blaring day and night. She needs a noisy home. She is on the telephone at all hours of the day and night and is a superb telephone communicator. She is "Dear Abby" to many women friends. She loves to hold parties, so we have periodic parties, dinners, and get-togethers at our home throughout the year.

Depot—Home is Like Grand Central Station

When the kids were growing up, our home was the gathering place for all of the kids in the neighborhood. Our home was like Grand Central Station. Karen would feed the neighborhood kids meals, provide a pantry full of junk food for their taking at any time, and provide them with all kinds of playthings (e.g., swimming pool, pool table, ping-pong table, foosball table, videocassette movies, and videogames).

Mushroom Cloud—Coming Out of My Shell

While they were growing up, Karen involved our kids in a myriad of activities including scouts, sports, piano, dance, acting, and you name it. I enjoyed being alone studying, working on my computer, or watching television. However, Karen involved me in all of our kids' activities, her parties, and other social events. She brought me out of my introverted shell and into the extroverts' realm.

Tunnel Rat—A Good Hermit

If it were not for Karen, I would be a hermit. In fact, Karen had once said that I would be a good hermit. I probably should have been a forest ranger stuck in a lookout tower way out in the jungles or hills somewhere gawking for forest fires. I could stay there for days on end by myself reading non-fiction books, writing books, listening to talk-radio, and watching *Fox News*. I would be perfectly content with that kind of life.

Torture—Forced Extroversion

However, because I had married an extrovert, that kind of life, obviously, was not for me. As the years went by, I have become more extroverted than otherwise. However, basically, that is a forced extroversion. I am shy, basically, but many people would never say that of me. However, that is my basic personality, and I know it. That is probably what contributed to my having a stuttering problem for over two decades of my life.

"Blood and Guts" Patton—Practicing What One Preaches

Upon practicing what I preach about networking, I have been able to accomplish the following:

- Acquired a consulting job through a close friend.
- Acquired four teaching jobs.
- Acquired other career jobs.
- Received awards and recognition through these close relationships.
- Elected and appointed to various organizational offices.
- Been involved in dozens of organizations (professional, educational, military, service, social, religious, and community). I was even a member of the Alpha Sigma Phi social fraternity. Got that? *Social* fraternity!
- Given hundreds and even up to over a thousand talks, speeches, sermons, training sessions, presentations, seminars, lessons, and workshops to small groups (under 10 people) and up to large conventions (hundreds and even up to a thousand people). Hermits do not do those things.

Fast Track—Working Areas of True Passion

Now, later in life, I am striving to work in my areas of true passion. This is why my career has migrated to the following endeavors:

- Teaching
- Researching
- Writing and publishing (books, articles, and papers)
- Consulting
- Career coaching
- Entrepreneurship

Victory—Self-actualization

These work activities match well with my INTJ personality. These are the areas where I am finding my greatest satisfaction and fulfillment. These are the areas where I can self-actualize. These are the areas where I will be involved with throughout the remainder of my life.

> ## Uda Bomb #28
>
> *To truly love what you do, you must do what you love.*
>
> **Richard Banfield**

Zealot—Find Your Passion

I encourage you to find your passion also and to network yourself so that you will capture jobs where you too can self-actualize. Richard Banfield said, "*To truly love what you do, you must do what you love.*"[32] And finally, Christopher Michel, CEO of Military.com, said, "*Networking is not an end in itself; it should be an enjoyable and interesting part of professional and personal development.*"[33]

---

[32] Richard Banfield, "Questions Every Potential Entrepreneur Should Ask," Crossroads Newsletter. (North Chelmsford, MA, Net-Temps, Inc., http://www.net-temps.com/, 2004), rmbanfield@udesignweprint.com.

[33] Christopher Michel, "Make Networking Work for You," Military.com, http://www.military.com, January 6, 2004.

Judy Rosemarin stated that the following steps can help reserved professionals become more effective networkers:

1. Recognize and deal with the aspects of networking that bother you most.
2. Create a structured plan, then stick to it.
3. Make calls when your energy is highest.
4. Know what you want to say when calling.
5. Take time out to replenish yourself.[34]

Assassination—Getting Ahead in the Corporate Jungle

I don't remember the class notes or the book talking about relying solely on oneself to get ahead in life. Your class and the book have focused on networking and getting to know others who can help you get ahead in life. If we were all so worried about ourselves, none of us would ever get ahead because the world would be full of selfish people.

Thank you for your very thoughtful question. Please understand that nowhere did I ever say that you needed to depend only on yourself to get ahead in "life." If I wrote or said that anywhere, I need you to show me exactly where I wrote or said that. Further, if it is true that I said or wrote that, I will retract that statement because I have never believed nor lived that.

Survival—Corporate Jungle

What I did say, however, is that if you are to get ahead and survive in the "corporate jungle," don't expect anyone (including your boss) to move you along the way you would expect to move up the corporation. In the corporate jungle, if you aren't looking out for yourself, i.e., number one, nobody else will be looking out for you. This is why I said that, in a corporation, everybody else seems also to be climbing the corporate ladder. I

---

[34] Judy Rosemarin, "Networking Strategies for Shy Professionals," *CareerJournal.com.* Extracted on 4/16/07 from http://www.careerjournal.com.

also said this: *Don't work for a boss or supervisor who is threatened by your superior, aggressive performance.* He/she won't help you at all if he/she is afraid of you taking away his/her job.

Patriot—No Company Loyalty

I also said this: Don't expect the company to show any loyalty to you. When layoff time comes around, if they need to cut heads and even though you may be the hardest working, loyal member of your group, you could still be laid off if your boss doesn't like you. Remember, I said that there were two reasons why companies will hire you: (1) they think you can help them make money and (2) they like you. You may be bringing in millions of dollars into the company as I was doing for a company for which I had worked. I was loyal to them, but was the company loyal to me? No! My boss feared what I was doing, i.e., making the company grow too fast. He didn't like that because he was losing control, and so he fired me. Where is the company loyalty to employees there? None! Zippo!

> **Uda Bomb #29**
>
> *Don't work for a boss or supervisor who is threatened by your superior, aggressive performance.*

Rambo—Be an Intrepreneur

This is why I said, in the corporate environment, we need to be thinking as an "intrepreneur," where we are our own boss of our own company (yes, even within a corporate structure). You need to think of yourself as "You, Inc." or "Me, Inc." as the article by Tom Peters, "The Brand Called You," talked about. You need to do your job as if you were running your own company. You need to differentiate yourself from your peers. You need subtly to self-promote yourself because nobody else will.

Al-Qaeda—Professional Jealousy

In a perfect world, we wouldn't need to worry about anyone stabbing us in the back. But as you start moving up in the corporation that you will some day call home, you will find that there are a lot of other employees competing for the same positions you are pursuing. You will meet up with people who will severely criticize you behind your back. They will throw figurative "rocks in your path." They will not help you on your projects and will, instead, try to make you look bad to your bosses. They will not be glad for you when you receive that promotion, raise, bonus, or award. They are jealous of you, particularly if you are a "mover and shaker," i.e., someone who gets things done. That's just the way it is in the corporate jungle.

Ally—Mutual Support

I also did say that you need to do job networking, and when you do get a job, you then need to do career networking (yes, within the corporate structure). This is where we mutually help each other to move ahead. Good networking nodes are people who help each other.

> # Uda Bomb #30
>
> *I'll scratch your back if you scratch mine.*

Thus, you'll need to be on the lookout for people whom you can trust and vice versa. Remember, I said, *"I'll scratch your back if you scratch mine."* That's hardly selfishness. That's mutual support. Lawyers like to call it a *quid pro quo* relationship, which means something for something.

Secular Progressives—Watch Out for Backstabbers

I'll tell you this: *You'll never get ahead in life if you don't depend on other people helping you along.* All I'm saying is for you to find those people who you can trust, and then, you all help each other to move forward, onward, and upward. Don't team up with a backstabber because that is just what that backstabber will do, i.e., stab you in the back, particularly when "push comes to shove." Backstabbers will never back you up. They will attempt to turn all the blame onto you, particularly if it is their fault. Hence, like anything else in life, we must select our friends and associates carefully. *Trust is the key ingredient in any successful relationship, even in a marriage.*

> ## Uda Bomb #31
>
> *You'll never get ahead in life if you don't depend on other people helping you along.*

Demilitarized Zone—The Gray Area

For being a questioning person, you deserve extra points. Stay that way throughout your entire life. You will discriminate yourself from the others. Never sit there and wonder about something. Question it. Contest it. Argue against it. Not many things in life are simply cut-and-dried. A gray area exists that always indicates that there may be room for another answer, a better answer, or an entirely different answer.

> ## Uda Bomb #32
>
> *Trust is the key ingredient in any successful relationship, even in a marriage.*

Please continue to question everything and anything I teach that you either disagree with or don't fully understand what I said or wrote. This is how we all grow. I want a class of students that question and challenge everything. By this process, we all become better people and workers.

Pre-emptive Strike—Getting to Know the Movers and Shakers

If you want to be a "mover and shaker," you need to know what they do and associate with them. Ross Macpherson wrote a good article that appeared in the April 11, 2005, issue of *JobSeekerWeekly* on learning how to get to know about and meeting "movers and shakers" in your industry. I say, *if you wanna be it, you gotta do it.*

Fast Trackers—Movers and Shakers

Macpherson wrote, "*The movers and shakers are those who stand at the pinnacle of the industry, who define where the industry is going, who understand the industry like no others, and who are tied in to everything that the industry is doing*. In other words, they are great networkers.

"Knowing the movers and shakers can do wonders for your networking and your career. If you are in their industry, or if you want to be, these are the people you need to know. The question is: How do you meet them?"

> ## Uda Bomb #33
>
> *The movers and shakers are those who stand at the pinnacle of the industry, who define where the industry is going, who understand the industry like no others, and who are tied into everything that the industry is doing.*
>
> **Ross Macpherson**

Macpherson wrote further, "Here are five of the best methods I know:

1. Read their articles
2. Become a member of professional associations
3. Attend conferences and introduce yourself to them
4. Communicate online with newsgroups, usenets, e-lists, or bulletin boards
5. Work on the right projects."[35]

One of the purposes of networking is to stand out from the pack. If you network successfully, you'll become known as the person who can be

---

[35] Ross Macpherson is the president of Career Quest, a certified professional resume writer and professional interview coach with over 12 years experience in career development and training. As an expert in "career marketing," Ross has helped thousands of professionals at all levels stand out from their competition and accelerate their career success through powerful resumes, job search techniques, and interviewing strategies.

counted on to remember birthdays, offer praise for a promotion, and is always just a phone call away.[36]

VIPs—Networking with High-level People

I corresponded with a deputy assistant level executive in the Clinton Administration once just by writing to him using his email address at the end of a magazine article he had written. I was quite impressed with what he wrote and told him in the email that I liked what he wrote. We corresponded back and forth several times.

> ### Uda Bomb #34
>
> *You too may network with people with whom you may never dream of networking.*

Again, I read an article in *Aerospace America*, the magazine of the American Institute of Aeronautics and Astronautics (AIAA), which was about the director general of Japan's equivalent of the NASA Kennedy Space Center (KSC) whose surname was the same as mine, i.e., Uda. Hence, I wrote to Dr. Hiroshi Uda, director general of the National Space Development Agency (NSDA) of Japan, Tsukuba Space Center (TSC), and wondered if we were related. He wrote to me several times and sent information and books. His father was the co-inventor of the Yagi-Uda antenna, and he even sent me a copy of his father's book on that antenna.

The point I make here, by relaying these two stories, is that you too can network with important people by just writing them, praising their work, or just have a "hook" as I did with Dr. Hiroshi Uda. Try it. *You too may network with people with whom you would never dream of networking.*

---

[36] Harvey Mackay, "Some Winning Strategies for Reluctant Networkers," *CareerJournal.com*. Extracted on 4/16/07 from http://www.careerjournal.com.

Chapter 5

Weapons of Mass Destruction—Secrets

S uccessful networking is based on building long-term relationships that can pay future dividends. The right way to network is to develop a proper attitude and habits. Stay in touch with people when you don't need anything. Do something for them, if you can.[37]

John DeFrancesco

Surveillance—Visibility Enhancement Effort (VEE)

Proactive Response—Make Things Happen

If you are not actively pursuing and making a concerted effort to network (meet and get to know people and vice versa) and to accomplish significant things to add to and enhance your resume, you are being "left in the dust" by your competitors. If you don't actively do these things in your career and life, things won't just automatically happen. You must make things happen.

Scribe—60-90-day VEE

To give you an idea of what I am talking about here, my VEE over a past 60-90-day period consisted of the following:

- Attended (networked) the spring 2005 Academic Assembly for faculty and academic administrators on 1/13/05 in ACD 102.

---

[37] John DeFrancesco, "The Value of Networking." *Public Relations Tactics*, March 2000, p. 22.

- Networked in meetings and other interactions with employees at L-3 Interstate Electronics Corporation (IEC) during a six-week proposal consulting gig in Anaheim.

- Continued networking in church and other meetings while serving as bishop of the Palomar Ward of young single adults. Attended Linger Longer dinners, bishop's firesides, ward family home evenings, activity nights, and temple assignments.

- Continued networking with students (getting to know some of them very well) while teaching a 16-week SSM 445 Career Development course at CSUSM.

- Attended (networked) August Williams' baptism on 2/12/05.

- Networked continuously and heavily with Dave Blackledge, VP operations of R.L. Phillips, Inc.

- Flew to Arizona on 2/25/05 to participate (networked) in grandson's ordination to the priesthood on 2/27/05 and attended dinner in son's friends' home (networked) before returning to California.

- Held telecom (networked) with close friend, Bill Billimoria, director of programs at BAE Systems in New York, who is suffering from cancer. He has many good connections in industry and has helped me before by giving me proposal consulting contracts.

- Visited (networked) with John Walsh, director of business development of Day & Zimmermann Defense Systems Group.

- Attended (networked) a brown bag seminar on "Cognitive Coaching as a Method of Mentoring" on 3/17/05 in the CSUSM Kellogg Library.

- Prepared and submitted nominations for the "Award for Outstanding Student Work in Community Service Learning" and "Award for Outstanding Service Learning Community Partner" to the Office of Community Service Learning (OCSL).

- Had networking lunch with Mr. Tarang Shah, product manager at Ericsson, Inc., and former direct report of mine when we had worked together at QUALCOMM, Inc.

- Met (networked) with Dr. Staci L. Beavers, director of the OCSL, to gather information to prepare an $800 grant application to perform Community Service Learning (CSL) research and possibly to prepare a $1,000 grant application to incorporate CSL into the SSM 445 Career Development course.

- Got to meet (networked) and know William Sheffield, a practicing attorney and former superior court judge.

- Attended (networked) the "Actively Managed Account" workshop at Asset Solutions, Inc., in San Diego on 3/26/05.

- Attended (networked) Dan Quinones baptism on 3/26/05 and attended party at his family's home thereafter.

- Had lunch (networked) with Steve Schaefer, former VP International and my former boss at Titan Wireless, Inc., at the Poseidon Restaurant in Del Mar on 3/29/05.

- Attended (networked) the "Grant Writing" workshop from 11:45 AM–1:00 PM in the Kellogg Library on 4/18/05.

- Attended (networked) the Brooke Porter—Steve Baker wedding on 4/23/05.

Interdiction—Meet the People

Show your plan for your VEE. In other words, what have you done and/or what are you planning to do to get yourself out in the public so that you get to meet/know more people and more people get to meet/know you? You need to go out and meet the people. Do it now!

Regime Change—Job Promotion

What do I need to do and how will I achieve what is necessary to be promoted in my career?

Invasion Force—Advancement

In your career, receiving a promotion is similar to earning an "A" in the "Career Development" course. It is no different from being the most popular person among your friends. It is no different than being elected to an office in the clubs and organizations you join. It is no different than being elected to a student body office. It is no different than being in demand by multiple companies when you do your job search. It is no different than receiving a reward or award for doing something beyond the usual.

Performance Appraisal—Reasons for Promotion

There are two reasons why an employer will hire you. You will make him/her money, and he/she likes you. Additionally, *there are two reasons why an employer will promote you. You do make him/her money, and he/she likes you.* There is no getting around it. You can make money for an employer, but if he/she dislikes you, you won't be promoted. On the other hand, an employer may like you, but if you don't make him/her any money, you also won't get promoted. Think about it. If you are not making the company money, you are only taking money out of the company with your salary or wage. Of course, if you don't make your employer any money and he/she dislikes you, you will be first on the layoff list.

> **Uda Bomb #35**
>
> *There are two reasons why an employer will promote you. You do make him/her money, and he/she likes you.*

Tactics—Approaches to Making Money

Thus, it is simple. Work to make your company money and do everything that makes your boss happy. That will improve your probability of receiving a promotion to around 90 percent. There are other things that equate to making money. Some of these things include the following:

- Saving money for the company
- Avoiding cost expenditures for the company
- Getting bookings for the company
- Improving productivity of the company
- Improving production efficiency for the company
- Acquiring new customers for the company
- Developing new tools and systems for the company that make products faster, cheaper, and better
- Bringing praise to the company for something wonderful that you have done
- Improving and maintaining customer satisfaction for the company
- Reducing company theft by apprehending or turning in employees who are robbing the company blind
- Improving company profitability
- Finishing jobs on schedule and within budget
- Creating new inventions for the company and receiving patents for your inventions
- Making new discoveries for the company
- Improving company processes
- Establishing programs that make the company and its employees better
- Improving the value of the company and improving the company's goodwill
- Adding value to the company's products and services
- Negotiating down subcontractor or supplier prices for purchased products and services
- Innovating ways of doing business for the company
- Generating positive press for the company in the media

Over-Excel—Above-and-Beyond the Call of Duty

All of these things make money for the company. So, whatever job you hold while working in any company, always look for things to do that will do any and all of the things shown in the above bullet list. Don't do things that just keep you busy but adds absolutely no value to the company. If you desire a promotion, you must be a mover and shaker in the company. You must add value. *You must do things above-and-beyond the call of duty.* You must make things happen. You must sacrifice for the company. You must be proactive instead of reactive. You must search for new and better things to do, not just wait for someone to tell you what to do.

> **Uda Bomb #36**
>
> *You must do things above-and-beyond the call of duty.*

Best of the Best: Top Gun—Be the Best That You Can Be

You need to network and get to know everyone in the company and vice versa. You need to let your boss know that you are seeking promotions, raises, bonuses, perks, and choice assignments. Then, go out and do things that qualify you for these promotions, raises, bonuses, perks, and choice assignments. *Be the best that you can be.* Keep your boss informed of all of the things you are accomplishing. Pursue and win awards and recognition. Work hard and do quality work. Show that you deserve promotions. Let people know what you want to do and where you want to be. Ask and you shall receive.

> **Uda Bomb #37**
>
> *Be the best that you can be.*

Net-centric Warfare (NCW)—Use Your Existing Grapevine

To open your eyes to career-change or promotional opportunities in your current environment, Janet Farley suggested to use your existing grapevine by doing the following:

- Generate interest in your qualifications.
- Review and revise your resume as necessary.
- Arrange for informal meetings with colleagues.
- Plan your job-search efforts as carefully as you would if you were unemployed.
- Establish your role within the grapevine.
- Visualize yourself in a different job at your employer.
- Improve your communication skills.
- Note and analyze the information flow throughout your company.
- Evaluate and revise your plan as necessary.[38]

Special Operations—Corporate Jungle

There are hundreds of other things I can tell you as to what you need to do to get promoted in your job. You can learn of other things you can do to get promoted by reading chapter 13, "Realities of the Corporate World," in my book titled *Career Quest for College Students: Career Development for Those Who Plan to Have a Successful Career.* Read it and learn what you can do to advance yourself in the corporate jungle.

---

[38] Janet I. Farley, "To Uncover Hidden Job Leads, Take Advantage of the Grapevine," *CareerJournal.com.* Extracted on 4/16/07 from http://www.careerjournal.com.

Interdiction—Should You Be a Reference for Anyone Who Asks You?

If someone asks you to give them a good reference even though you know they are a terrible employee, what should you do?

Slackers—No Reference for Lousy Workers

If someone is a lousy performer, turn him/her down flat. Remember, you place your own reputation on the line whenever you give someone a good reference that is undeserved. It is best to tell that person that you prefer not to give him/her a reference than to try to fake one. You will not come across as genuine. You'll just end up with "egg on your face."

Crack Forces—Reference for Deserving People

I will give a good reference on anyone who is outstanding and would prove me to be right when I extol his/her virtues to any potential employer. If I wouldn't hire that person myself, I wouldn't give him/her a reference. For me to want to hire you, you must be a hard worker, producer, and outstanding performer.

Turncoats—No Reference for Backstabbers

I would never give references to some students in each of my classes. Those who I cannot trust because they are backstabbers, those who badmouth me to others, those who do a lousy job in my classes, and those who lack integrity will never get a reference from me. Never!

Rumor Mill—Grapevine Never Fails

If anyone badmouths me to others, the word always gets back to me because I always have loyal friends who will tell me about those backstabbers. Hence, if you are one of these kinds of people, don't ever ask for a reference from me or from anyone else for that matter. You will go through life being known as a backstabber. The grapevine never fails.

Fellow Traveler—Don't Lie for Liars

I had a consultant that worked for me once who asked me if I would give him a reference. Because he did a good job for me on that particular job, I said I would. Then, he asked me if I would vouch that he had worked over a period that he didn't work for me. In other words, he asked me to lie for him. I then flatly told him that I would not lie for him in a reference call. He disappeared with his tail between his legs.

Evasive Action—Shun Liars

It just irks me when someone asks me to lie for them. What kind of a person of integrity is he to ask me to lie? He totally lacks integrity. He can lie for himself, but I won't lie for him. If you are used to being a liar, then you can lie for others.

> ## Uda Bomb #38
>
> *Liars are the worst kind of rats to work for or to have working for you. Shun them.*

However, for me, don't ever insult me by asking me to lie for you. *Liars are the worst kind of rats to work for or to have working for you. Shun them.*

Sabotage and Dirty War—Burning Bridges

Offensive—Oversensitive Student

I had an oversensitive student who took offense because I had the student's name on a list of seven people who had not checked in with me by email in response to an email that I had sent to the entire class. Here is what this student wrote in an email to me:

> *Currently I have three jobs and am working hard. Sorry if I do not check my email every day. It sounds to me like you have too much time on your hands. I do not appreciate your list singling me, and implying that I am a slacker. So far, you are off to the wrong foot. It is summer VACATION; leave me alone.*

[Ed. From past experience, there is one like this in every group, crowd, or class. My response follows below.]

Measured Response—My Response

Hi So-and-So,

Thank you for your candid feedback. If you are not a slacker as you say you aren't, you have nothing to be concerned about. Every other student in the class replied positively to my emails. I have three jobs too, so I know how hard you are working.

You misread my email. I am not expecting any of you to check your email daily during the summer break. However, when the semester starts, I suggested that everyone check his/her email daily, but the hard requirement is to check it at least once a week.

I have only 24 hours in a day on my hands, just as you and everyone else, so I don't have, as you say, "too much time on my hands." The list did not single you out. It just listed the seven students who have not yet responded to my initial email.

I'm sorry that you took offense by my listing you as one of those seven who have yet to respond. During the course of the semester, as people miss deadlines for submitting assignments, I will again be listing the names of those who are tardy. So, if you are going to be upset at my listing your name as one missing a deadline, please don't be late on any of your assignments. That way, you won't again take offense if your name is on a list.

Since this is summer vacation, rest assured, I will leave you alone, as you suggested, by taking your name off the distribution list for anything I send out to the class as information. I will put you back on the distribution list the Saturday before the start of the fall semester. So, please don't worry about being bothered any longer this summer. :-)

So-and-so, I appreciate your email. If you are a good student as you imply, I want you to stay in the class. I look forward to meeting you on the first day of class on Tuesday, August 30th. As a unique individual, I expect you to be one of the top students in my class … if not THE top student. See you on August 30!

Sincerely,

Bob Uda
Adjunct Faculty Lecturer

I wish I had that intestinal fortitude to sit in judgment of my professors when I went to college during the stone ages. We certainly live in a different world today.

Massacre — Contingency Planning

Reinforcements — Contingency Plan

Personal contact allows you to probe more directly about a particular job or company and establish how well the fit for this position would be with your skills, knowledge, and abilities. However, you need a contingency plan if the company absolutely does not want you to call, visit, or contact anyone in the firm.

Security Classification — Top Secret Ideas

Do you know about the "Don't call us; we'll call you" syndrome? I have probed many ideas regarding defeating this syndrome … even against the wishes of the company. These TOP SECRET ideas include the following:

- Find out the names, titles, phone numbers, and addresses of key executives in the company and contact them (using both snail mail and email)
- Get your resume into the hands of a friend in the company, and he/she will get it into the right hiring manager's hands
- Visit a friend or acquaintance in that company and work it so that he/she informally introduces you to the hiring manager

Chapter 6
Armageddon — Results

*N*OW *more than ever, networking is crucial to your success. So make the most of Baylor Career Services because NETWORKING is what we do!*[39]

Matt Harris
Graduate Student
Baylor MBA Career Services

Apocalypse — Conclusions

Networking is the most important technique for finding a good job and for advancing rapidly in your career. Hone your networking skills and you will be successful in all of your career endeavors.

Be a Good Networking Node

Treaty—A Two-way Affair. Being a good networking node requires "receiving" and subsequent "giving." It is a two-way affair. It is not a one-way affair as many students think. I really believe that they do not understand the concerted effort it requires to be a good networking node. If people will not uphold their side of the networking bargain, then I don't want them as a networking node. It is as simple as that!

Reading the Enemy—Those Who Get It. Only about five or six students in each of my classes ever qualify to be good networking nodes because

---

[39] Matthew Harris, "Was Your Dad a 'Company Man'?" *Baylor Business Review*, Spring-Summer 2000, p. 32.

73

they learn and understand the obligation of the unspoken reciprocity required whenever they receive help. These people will go far in their careers and in life in general. I want to keep tabs of these people throughout their careers.

Return Fire—Reciprocity is Key. Most people do not ever learn how to be good networking nodes because, basically, they are selfish and only want to receive but never ever think of giving back anything. The only reciprocity they think of and do is to screw you. What kind of networking node does that make them? With friends like that, who needs enemies!

Game Plan—Baseball Analogy

Point Man—Stepping Into the Batter's Box. Baseball is the only major sport in which the defensive team initiates the action. The game doesn't start until the ball is delivered from the pitcher. Offense begins by stepping up to the plate. When you think about it, the same is true when networking for a new position. To reach contacts and secure referrals, you must step into the batter's box. You may strike out at first, but eventually you'll hit a home run that leads to the job you want. [40]

Skirmishes—Strikeouts are Mandatory. Don't lose heart if you step up [to] the plate, swing and miss—repeatedly. Striking out is part of the game, but sitting on the bench means watching the game go by. Remember that baseball's leading hitters make successful contact only 3 times out of 10. They also step up to the plate more than 500 times a year. [41]

Continued Attack—Be Persistent. Years ago, an entrepreneur had a similar experience. To finance his dream project, he visited 301 banks, which all denied his request for capital. But an officer at the 302nd bank said, "OK, we'll help you build your theme park, Mr. Disney." Perseverance paid off for Walt Disney and will pay off for job seekers as well. [42]

---

[40] Matthew Harris, "Was Your Dad a 'Company Man'?" *Baylor Business Review*, Spring-Summer 2000, p. 32.

[41] Ibid.

[42] Ibid.

Nuclear Holocaust—Recommendations

To capture and keep great jobs, I recommend you do the following:

- Consider networking as the most important tool in your job search toolbox.
- Develop your networking skills by learning and practicing all of the ideas discussed in this book.
- Learn about and be an excellent networking node.
- Seek out good networking nodes to keep in contact with throughout your life.
- Maintain your good networking nodes and relationships throughout your life.
- Be responsive and helpful to your best networking nodes … always.
- Prepare and send letters of references as soon as possible after a good networking node asks you for a reference letter.

When you look for a job, perform job or employment networking. When you land a job, continue with career networking. If you will network throughout your life, you will receive a lot more benefits than otherwise. Good luck!

About the Author

R obert T. (Bob) Uda is president, owner, general manager, and principal consultant of Bob Uda and Associates (BU&A). He had served in the United States Air Force for over eight years and in the aerospace and defense industries for over a quarter century. He has also worked in the software services, wireless telecommunications, information technology, and electronics industries for seven years. Hence, he has a total of over 40 years of professional working experience in the military, aerospace/defense, and other industries.

Bob Uda currently serves as proposal center manager of BAE Systems, Inc., Network Systems (NS) Line of Business. Bob has served as director of business capture and proposal development of Ocean Systems Engineering Corporation (OSEC); manager of proposal development of L-3 Communications Interstate Electronics Corporation (IEC); director of marketing and proposals at Titan Wireless, Inc.; and manager of business processes, project manager-IT, and senior manager of proposal development at QUALCOMM, Inc.

Furthermore, he served as chairman, president, and CEO of Apollo Systems Technology, Inc.; vice president and general manager at North American Manufacturing Corporation; vice president of business development at Sterling Software, Inc.; and general manager, product line manager, and program manager at HR Textron Inc.

At Rockwell International Space Systems Division, Bob served as project manager, program development manager, manager of advanced programs (proposal development), and member of the technical staff. Furthermore, he served as deputy program manager (project engineer) at TRW Defense and Space Systems Group and astronautical development engineer in the USAF.

Bob earned BS degrees in aerospace engineering from the University of Oklahoma and in general business from Regents College of the University of the State of New York (now named Excelsior College). He further earned an MS degree in astronautics from the Air Force Institute of Technology (AFIT) and an MBA degree from the University of La Verne (California). Furthermore, he received a diploma in The Executive Program in Management from the UCLA Graduate School of Management. Currently, Bob works on an online PhD degree in Business Administration (BA) with specialization in Homeland Security (HS) from the Northcentral University (NCU) located in Prescott Valley, Arizona, and plans to graduate at the end of 2010. He serves as president and as a member of the Student Advisory Board (SAB) at NCU.

An award-winning writer, Bob has written/published over 40 publications including 13 books — 7 of them related to career development (including this book). He has served as a full-time professor of systems acquisition management with the Defense Acquisition University (DAU) and taught courses covering program management, systems engineering, and systems acquisition management. As an adjunct faculty lecturer, he taught "Career Development" in the College of Business Administration at the California State University San Marcos. He taught "Writing and Publishing" as an instructor in the Osher Lifelong Learning Institute Program at Cal State San Marcos Office of Extended Studies. Furthermore, he taught logistics graduate students as an adjunct faculty member of National University.

He is a fellow in the British Interplanetary Society (BIS), associate fellow in the American Institute of Aeronautics and Astronautics (AIAA), Certified Manager (CM) with the Institute of Certified Professional Managers (ICPM), and a founding charter member of the Association of Proposal Management Professionals (APMP). He also serves as vice chairman of the board and an at-large member of the ICPM Board of Regents (BOR). Furthermore, he serves as a director and vice president of the International Technology Institute (ITI). Additionally, Bob is a member of the International Association for Counterterrorism and Security Professionals (IACSP), member of the International Association of Law Enforcement Intelligence Analysts, Inc. (IALEIA), associate member of the International Counter Terrorism Officers Association (ICTOA), and member of the National Defense Industrial Association (NDIA).

He was the District 12 Write-up Winner as well as the State Write-up Winner in the California Jaycees. Along with co-authors Dr. Istvan Tuba and Dr. Anthony Etele, Bob received a Certificate of Excellence as a finalist in the Best Published Non-fiction Books of 2005, Politics and Social Science category, with their book titled *The Third Resource: A Universal Ideology of Economics* at The 12th Annual San Diego Book Awards sponsored by the San Diego Book Awards Association, Inc., on May 20, 2006.

In November 2007, he received the Honorable Mention award in the Maritime Security Expo (MSE) and Northcentral University (NCU) paper competition. His paper was titled "Detecting and Defeating Waterborne Improvised Explosive Devices (WBIEDs) Onboard Small Vessels."

Internationally recognized in community service, Bob appears in 46 Who's Who publications including *Who's Who in the World, Who's Who in America, Who's Who in California, Who's Who in Science and Engineering,* and *Who's Who in Finance and Industry.*

Bob Uda was born in Honolulu, Hawaii, and lived in Hawaii for 20 years. He is the third of seven children of Masao and Irene Kuualoha Uda (both deceased). In the 45 years since leaving Hawaii, he has lived in Oklahoma, Ohio, Florida, Connecticut, and California with short stints in Utah, Alabama, Massachusetts, Texas, and Washington.

Bob and his wife, the former Karen Elizabeth Rowland of Circleville, Ohio, sired two sons, a daughter, and four grandchildren. They live in San Marcos, California. You can contact Bob by e-mail at bobuda@roadrunner.com.

Index

978-0-595-47949-8
0-595-47949-9